Table of Contents

It's a Spider!

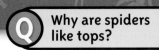
What has eight legs, fangs, and hair all over?

Is it a monster? No. It's a spider!

Some of us are afraid of creepy-crawly spiders.

But most spiders can't hurt people.

Web Word

FANG:
A biting mouthpart of a spider or a large, sharp tooth in other animals

5

Spiders, Spiders Everywhere!

Spiders live in deserts and rain forests.
They live on mountains and plains.

They live on beaches and in caves.
Spiders live almost anywhere.

A Spider's Body

Spiders can
be big or small.
They can be
brown or black.

Some spiders
are red, orange,
green, or yellow!

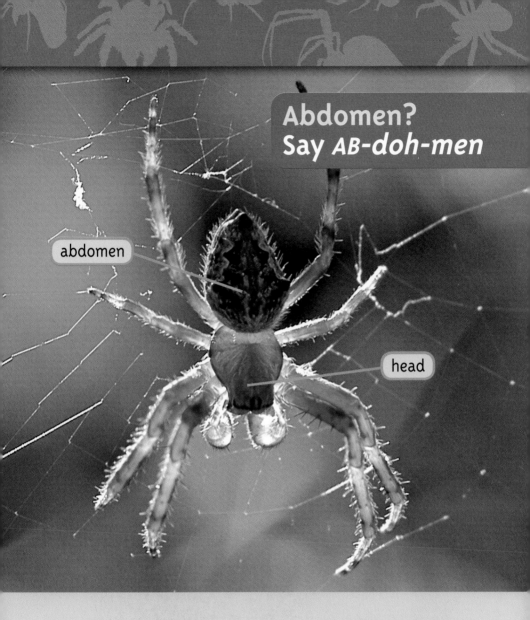

Abdomen?
Say *AB-doh-men*

abdomen

head

They may come in different colors.
But all spiders have eight legs. And
they all have two main body parts—
a head and an abdomen.

Spider Food

spider

insect

Q What does a spider do when he gets angry?

A He goes up a wall!

All spiders are meat-eaters.
Most spiders eat insects.

Some spiders eat bigger animals
like fish, snakes, lizards, or frogs.

Sometimes spiders even eat
each other!

spider

frog

Spiders have fangs that hold venom. Venom kills the prey or keeps it from moving.

But spiders don't have teeth to chew their food.

They suck the liquids out of their prey. Yummy!

Web Word

VENOM: Poison
PREY: An animal that is eaten by other animals

fangs

Senses

Most spiders have eight eyes.
But they can't see very well.

So they need more than their eyes
to catch dinner.

Small hairs on a spider's legs sense movement. A spider feels an insect caught in its web. It's dinnertime!

Web Builders

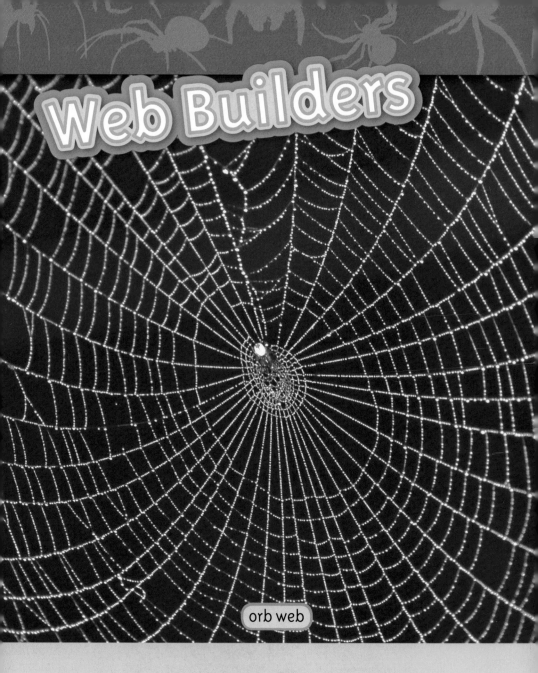

orb web

Different spiders make different webs.
Orb webs have a circle pattern.

funnel web

tangle web

trap-door spider's web

Funnel webs are built like tubes.

Tangle webs (cobwebs) are a jumble of threads.

Trap-door spider webs cover a spider's home in the ground.

Spinning Silk

Not all spiders make webs. But all spiders make silk.

They wrap their eggs in silk. They wrap their prey in silk, too.

Spiders even travel by silk! They use it like a rope. Spiders climb down to different places. Or they let the wind carry them.

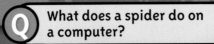
Q What does a spider do on a computer?

A It works on its own web site!

A spider wrapping its prey in silk

Super Spiders!

Check out these really cool spiders from all over the world.

Strangest

Bolas spider
It catches its prey with sticky thread, as if fishing.

Goliath birdeater tarantula

It's so big, it can eat young birds. It lives in South America.

Biggest

Most Famous

Black widow

It is the most poisonous spider in North America. It sometimes eats its mate.

Brazilian wandering spider

It shows its red jaws when angry. It lives in South and Central America.

Deadliest

Best Leaper

Jumping spider

It stalks its prey. It leaps huge distances to pounce on its lunch.

Darwin's bark spider

It makes the world's largest webs—as big as two city buses!

Best Weaver

Best Mother

Wolf spider

She's a fierce predator but a careful mother. She carries her babies on her back!

Baby Spiders

Big or small, all spiders start out as eggs. A mother spider protects her eggs in an egg sac.

eggs

egg sac

Some spiders lay up to 2,000 eggs.

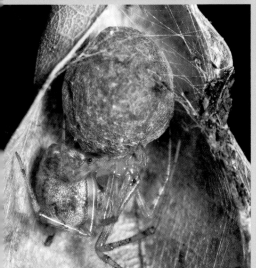

She may keep the egg sac safe on a web, under a leaf, or in a log.

She may carry her egg sac with her, too.

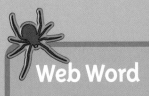

Web Word

EGG SAC:
A silk pouch that protects and holds spider eggs

The spider
eggs hatch!

Baby spiders
crawl out to
meet the
world. They
are called
spiderlings.

Helpful Spiders

Spiders are helpful to have around.

Their silk is super strong. It's light and stretchy. People are finding new ways to use spider silk.

Fabric made from spider silk

Spiders also eat biting bugs such as mosquitoes.

Let's hear it for spiders! Hooray!

What in the World?

These pictures show close-up views of spidery things. Use the hints below to figure out what's in the pictures. Answers on page 31.

HINT: This is a usual spider hangout.

HINT: If you had eight of these, you could do many things at once!

WORD BANK

legs   silk   egg sac   web   fangs   eyes

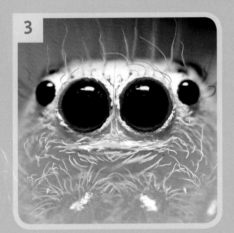

HINT: More of these don't help spiders. Our two work better.

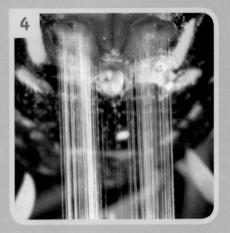

HINT: Spiders don't drink milk. But they make something that rhymes with it.

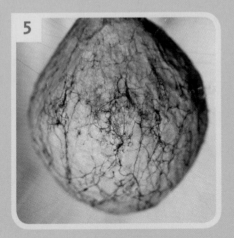

HINT: Rock-a-bye-baby . . . Spiders' eggs are kept safe in this.

HINT: Ouch! These can give a nasty bite.

Answers: 1. web, 2. legs, 3. eyes, 4. silk, 5. egg sac, 6. fangs

31

Glossary

EGG SAC: A silk pouch that protects and holds spider eggs

FANG: A biting mouthpart of a spider or a large, sharp tooth in other animals

PREY: An animal that is eaten by other animals

VENOM: Poison